POURING MY HEART OUT!

RAKHI HARIDAS

Contents

About the Author..5

Acknowledgements 7

01. Unexpected Bestie!.. 9

02. Soulmate! 11

03. Defeat the Its! 13

04. The Four Values of Life 15

05. Gratitude 17

06. The Happy Dancer 21

07. The Reunited Angels 23

08. Hope 25

09. Humans.. 27

10. A Bird 29

11. Mother.. 31

12. Favourite 33

13. My Daddy 35

14. Listen to Me 37

Contents

15. Rain... 39

16. Skills.. 41

17. There or Not?... 43

18. Smile.. 45

19. The Day... 47

20. Tolerance... 49

21. Kiddos... 51

About the Author

Rakhi Haridas is a Bangalore-based IT professional and a Kuchipudi dancer.

Pouring My Heart Out is a collection of her thoughts, what matters to her, and what she wishes to convey to her readers.

Acknowledgements

To the Almighty who guided me through each line I wrote,

To my mentor, who drives me, convinces me, inspires me,

To my parents, who encouraged me to write and gave feedback,

To my sister, who motivates, scolds and criticises my lines,

And to all who were part of this journey in various capacities,

I am beyond grateful to each one of you.

01

Unexpected Bestie!

While I was in the dark,
He came into my life like a spark!
He encouraged me to speak out,
But I was still in doubt!
He inspired me to the highest,
Slowly, I trusted him to the fullest.
He showed me new views on life,
And I could relate without any strife;
He told me to fight,
Instead of pondering over my plight,
My buried skills he found,
And I am now a hound.
I am a happy person now,
Chasing my passion and dreams avow,
I am in the light,
Looking towards my future bright.

02

Soulmate!

I knew she was on the way
I looked forward to her anyway.
There she came amidst us
I thought she would create a fuss,
I loved to play with her,
But at times, to do a war,
She grew up being mischievous
While I chose to be soundless,
She hated comparison with me
But always looked forward to me,
I was always busy
But she always waited calmly,
She loved her books
With which she became hooks.
I moved on with my life
Not much worried about her site,
Life had thrown its tantrums
Then I realised I needed her shoulders.
I ran back to her

And she tightly held me onto her,
Now, we started the same old war
But with more love and play than ever,
She is my lifeline,
She is my soulmate,
Yes, she is my sister!

03

Defeat the Its!

It looks attractive, It looks promising, It looks harmless;
You enter with hope, and you trust it to bring you good.

You put your baby steps into it, you look around, you are
perplexed,
It is not how you perceive it, and it is not what you
expected.

It throws challenges at you, everything in its own way,
You try to manage, you try to adjust, you try to change.

It mocks you, it hurts you, it laughs at you, it loves to see
you fall,
You saw its true colours, and you realised it to be different.

You cannot fall, you cannot fail, you cannot be mocked,
It is not above you, and it is not powerful enough to erase
your abilities.

You rise above it, you stand up for yourself, you show it,
It sees your power, it sees your courage, and it looks at you
in awe.

Now it adjusts, now it accepts you as you, it doesn't have a
choice,
It walks along with you, it supports you, it encourages you.

It can be your friends, It can be your relations, it can be
anyone, it can be anything,
It is your life, and that is how it is.

Stay away from it when it wants to pull you down
When you stand up, it will change sides and come with
you.

Don't change for any of it, don't push away your abilities,
Hold on to your conscience, and trust your inner self; it
never cheats.

Rise above all; you are more beautiful than all of it!
Rise above all; you are more powerful than all of it!
Rise above all; you are more daring than all of it!

04

The Four Values of Life

Completing your education	over	Falling in Love!
Becoming Financially independent	over	Getting Married!
Being Yourself	over	Adjusting for Others!
Prioritising Mental Health	over	Pleasing Everyone!

Disclaimer: While there is value in items on the right, I recommend following the items on the left more for a healthy, peaceful and happy life :-) - for both men and women!!!

Inspired by the Agile Manifesto!!!

05

Gratitude

What really matters?

At all times, we are busy
Running after success, fame and money.

At all times, we are busy
Living to fulfil the expectations of others.

At all times, we are busy
Finding out why we are not happy.

At all times, we are busy
Stressing out thinking about the future.

Does it really matter?

Every time, ask yourself
What blessings do I have?

Every time, ask yourself
Who do I have with me?

Every time ask yourself
Why am I given this life?

Every time ask yourself
Am I doing justice to myself?

That's all that matters!

Be grateful for your life,
Be grateful for your health,
Be grateful for your people,
Be grateful for yourself.

You are special,
You are beautiful,
You are skilled,
You are blessed!

And That's All That Matters!

Being grateful brings you fame!
Being grateful brings you success!
Being grateful brings you peace!

Being grateful brings you happiness!

Change your attitude; <u>Embrace Gratitude!</u>

06

The Happy Dancer

My body moved when I heard music,
My legs tapped when I heard music,
My heart rejoiced when I moved my body,
My mind was full when I tapped my legs.

I watched many others who did the same;
I was delighted equally as when I did it
I realised it was dancing,
I realised it was dancing!

I got lucky to learn it,
I got lucky to feel it,
I got lucky to observe it,
I got lucky to perform it,

I realised its various forms,
I learnt a few from many
I liked one the most;
I wanted to immerse in my interest.

Grateful to my mentors who shaped me
Grateful to my parents, who supported me
Grateful to my well-wishers who loved me
Grateful to be a dancer, and continue to be one.

07

The Reunited Angels

Amidst the city, we met at the abode of angels,
Innocent and lovely each little angel looked.

Few smiled, few cried, few were confused,
There was a guide to make us comfortable.

All angels grew up, gaining wisdom, exploring around,
We faced challenges, competitions, fights and friendships.

We loved our abode, we loved our guides,
We loved our playgrounds, we loved our trees and flowers.

It was time to leave our abode; it was goodbye time,
All angels flew out with rich experience.

Angels got busy with life, got immersed in duties,
As years passed, slowly got connected remotely.

All angels realised the same connection,
All angels got overwhelmed with joy.

Came the thought of reuniting once again,
Came the idea of meeting on the Silver Jubilee.

Angels came together, met each other,
Love and smiles flew throughout.

Angels did not feel the distance,
Angels expressed life experiences.

Few angels who touched the Lord's feet were remembered,
Few angels still are away, waiting to be united.

Angels pledged to meet more often,
Angels promised to be there forever for each other.

Here we are - the REUNITED ANGELS.

08

Hope

It is needed when you are broken,
It is needed when you are in doubt.

It is needed when you struggle,
It is needed when you fail.

It is needed when you are cheated,
It is needed when you see injustice.

It is needed when you are turned off,
It is needed when you feel alone.

It is needed when you are in the dark,
It is needed when you are helpless.

Who will give it to me?
Where will I find it?

It comes from within, and it resides in your inner self,
It is your strength that you have not noticed.

You find it, you get amazed,
You find it, and you see it's strength.

It tells you, "you are wonderful,"
It tells you, "you deserve success."

It tells you, "you are beautiful,"
It tells you, "you are complete."

It tells you, "you are the best,"
It tells you, "you are secure."

It tells you, "you are intense,"
It tells you, "you are invincible."

It tells you, "you are gentle,"
It tells you, "you are fast."

It tells you, "all is well,"
It tells you, "all will be well."

09

Humans

Complex, good and bad, kind and cruel,
Difficult to predict, unable to judge.

Can see compassionate ones, pure souls,
Also, deal with cunning ones, immoral and impure.

Sometimes lovely, caring, tender and warm,
At times, egoistic, heartless, indifferent and malevolent.

Each one unique, impossible to change,
Be the change that you like to see.

Ignore flaws, spread love, forget and forgive,
Meanwhile, ensure not being taken for granted.

Trust the universe, believe in good,
Being humane is not rare; humanity still exists.

10

A Bird

I opened my eyes,
I saw my Mamma,
She fed me
She loved me
She taught me to fly.

I loved her much
I loved my nest,
I lived happily,
Then, I was caught
And I was caged.

I was away from Mamma,
I was away from my nest,

A small girl caged me,
She loved me,
But I loved freedom;
She fed me too

But I loved Mamma,
She talked to me,
But I loved my nest.

Her friend came too
She saw me, adored me;
I was not enjoying it.
One day, my cage was open
I saw the friend asking me to fly
I flew away, thanking her.

I came back to my nest,
I came back to Mamma,
I enjoyed freedom again,
I told Mamma,
"Not all humans are bad!"

11

Mother

She was happy to know about me
She waited patiently to see my face

I troubled her so much before showing my face
She endured all that and patiently waited.

I was loved unconditionally,
I was given all the care and affection.

She nurtured me, she taught me,
She found all my skills and encouraged me.

She ensured I was perfect,
She promised she would be there.

She overlooked her happiness,
She always thought about others.

She is my mummy
She sacrifices herself for us

I want you to relax
I want you to do what you couldn't so far.

I want you to love yourself, too!

12

Favourite

When did you become my favourite?
I don't remember, I am sorry.

Being a fussy toddler, nothing amused me;
In my teen hood, you grabbed my attention.

Then I fell in love, deeply and badly,
I tried being away but in vain.

Slowly saw and realised your many faces,
But the first simple one remained my favourite.

I travelled around, still looking for you,
Caught you wherever you were hiding.

You cannot escape; you will always be my favourite,
Though they tease me, I can be with you throughout.

I love you Dosa :-) I always love you,
You make me happy, and you give me satisfaction.

I love you Dosa; wherever I go,
You are my favourite food!

13

My Daddy

He was away when I came
But I knew him through my post uncle.

Uncle brought me toys and chocolates
Saying, "your daddy has sent them!"

When he came, I was running around
I made sure he never went back.

Then I grew up with him,
Along with my sister, who joined me.

He saved us always from Mamma's scoldings
He gave us anything we asked for!

He was kind and patient
Not only with us, but with anyone around!

A few did take his kindness for granted;
They grabbed from him what he owned.

But Daddy remained cool
He showed us patience is a virtue!

I love him for his calmness,
I love him for his patience.

He was very naughty when we grew up
So, Daddy, we are with you, same as you cared for us.

14

Listen to Me

You come to this world,
You are the apple of the eye for all

You are loved, adored,
You are given everything around.

You grow up happily, freely
And you are a girl.

Now, entering womanhood,
Starts all the 'don'ts' around you.

Don't talk loud, don't sit with your legs up,
Don't be out with your friends for long.

All for going into another house
All for entering a different home.

For making it your own,
For nurturing new humans.

Do it, do it with all your heart,
Without ignoring yourself.

Be independent in opinions,
Be independent in finances.

Be your own in choices,
Be your self at all times.

Listen to ME, my dear women,
Listen to ME for taking charge of your life!

15

Rain

Dark clouds, announce your coming
A Happy me smiled when I was a child.

I loved the drizzles, the calm pouring;
I Desired to play with you, always.

At times, you throw down heavily,
Making sure we are all drenched fully.

Sometimes I hate you, showing your anger,
Giving trouble to earth, taking away our belongings.

In summer, we pray for you to come
And when you come in full strength, we fear you.

Please don't destroy us; our lives matter,
Come with love and shower your kindness on us.

We love you, we need you for living,
So don't show your might; we cannot bear it.

I want to smile when I think of you,
Without stress on the outcomes.

So come with a smile, come gently
Come always, bring us life.

Everyone needs you; we wait for you
And We promise to respect nature!

16

Skills

They hide within; you never know;
You have it all in you; you never know.

I thought I could not cook, but that wasn't true,
I thought I could not draw, but that wasn't true.

I thought I always needed someone,
I thought I could not be alone.

You overlook your abilities,
You overlook your strengths.

I realised the importance of giving it a try
Only to understand the skills are spry.

All skills lie within us,
All capabilities are within us.

I can do anything I really wish to,
I can upskill myself to do anything I want to.

Trust yourself, believe in yourself,
You are capable of anything and everything.

17

There or Not?

Little me heard many stories about you,
Also heard many names that you had.

Somehow, I felt it was funny,
I believed it was all fake.

I grew up and liked your stories,
Always read and watched things about you.

I felt sometimes you are there,
You tried to give me a nudge when i was alone.

I enjoyed it, but I am still not sure if it was you
I liked it, even if it was just my feeling.

Do I believe you exist?
Do I trust you are there?

I am not sure; still, I don't know,
Maybe you are there, well, among us.

Do ghosts exist? Do spirits stay back?
Are you happy here if you do?

No answers I have, only stories I hear,
No proof I have, only thoughts and feelings.

Maybe you are there, Maybe you are not!

18

Smile

An upward curve of your lips,
A strong symbol of life.

A contagious expression,
A powerful healer.

It makes a stranger approachable,
It makes your dull day brighter.

It gives someone hope,
It gives someone the courage.

When you give it, it comes back,
So give it in abundance; our world needs it.

It acts as medicine,
It also takes the form of appreciation.

It also acknowledges and makes someone happy,
It shows that you care; it puts someone at ease.

Don't hesitate to spread it,
Don't count it, let it flow.

Smile even when you are sad,
For it comes back to make you happy.

Your smiling face will be remembered,
Your smile's effects will stay.

19

The Day

The day I came into the world,
The day I smiled,
The day I stood up,
The day I walked.

The day I talked,
The day I went to school,
The day I got friends,
The day I liked books.

The day I danced,
The day I performed,
The day I passed exams,
The day I found my passion.

The day I got a job,
The day I felt love,
The day I had my family,
The day I had a child.

The day I was humiliated,
The day I endured,
The day I ignored,
The day I suffered.

The day I realised self-love,
The day I knew priorities,
The day I decided,
That's the day it all changed.

Today, I smile; I have friends and family,
Today, I put myself first,
Today, I stay away from negativity,
Today I am happy!!!

20

Tolerance

I belong to all living beings,
The belonging is equal,
Humans, animals, birds and insects,
The share is equal.

My dear beings, please pause;
It is time for a short reflection,
I realise a trigger,
Dangerous enough to break me.

Each one of you is important to me,
Even when you have different opinions,
Each one of you makes me complete,
Even when you have different perspectives.

When you see differences,
When you hear differences,
When you realise differences,
Why don't you accept fellow beings as they are?

Acceptance is a virtue; learn from me
As Mother Earth I hold all of you
Without showing a difference to any;
Be the same to the beings around you.

Respect the differences, accept the choices,
Enhance tolerance; trust me, it's important!

21

Kiddos

Lovely to see, awesome to cuddle,
Look at their smile, and then you also smile.

Rolling over, showing their gums,
Stealing hearts all around.

Curious minds explore in all ways,
Learn fast and teach us new things.

Watch them and see wonders,
Observe them and learn.

Listen to them and be awestruck,
See the different perspectives.

They love to be heard
They want attention and respect.

Show them right and wrong,
Show them good and bad.

Forcing does not work,
Giving experience does.

Look at the wonders when you trust them
Look at the wonders when you are there for them.

· · ·

www.ingramcontent.com/pod-product-compliance
Lightning Source LLC
Chambersburg PA
CBHW020514160726
47991CB00007B/2941